mj

PRIUS

Daniel Benjamin

Marshall Cavendish
Benchmark
New York

Published by Marshall Cavendish Benchmark
An imprint of Marshall Cavendish Corporation

Other Marshall Cavendish Offices:
Marshall Cavendish International (Asia) Private Limited, 1 New Industrial Road, Singapore 536196 • Marshall Cavendish International (Thailand) Co Ltd. 253 Asoke, 12th Flr, Sukhumvit 21 Road, Klongtoey Nua, Wattana, Bangkok 10110, Thailand • Marshall Cavendish (Malaysia) Sdn Bhd, Times Subang, Lot 46, Subang Hi-Tech Industrial Park, Batu Tiga, 40000 Shah Alam, Selangor Darul Ehsan, Malaysia

Marshall Cavendish is a trademark of Times Publishing Limited

All websites were available and accurate when this book was sent to press.

Library of Congress Cataloguing-in-Publication Data

Elish, Dan.
Prius / by Daniel Benjamin.
p. cm. — (Green cars)
Includes bibliographical references and index.
Summary: "Provides information about the hybrid technology used in the Prius, and discusses how the green movement is affecting the auto industry"–
Provided by publisher.
ISBN 978-1-60870-011-0
1. Prius automobile — Juvenile literature. I. Title.
TL215.P78E35 2011
629.22'93 — dc22
2009035463

Editor: Megan Comerford
Publisher: Michelle Bisson
Art Director: Anahid Hamparian
Series Designer: Daniel Roode

Illustrations on pp. 18–19 and p. 28 by Alanna Ranellone

Photo Research by Connie Gardner

Cover photo by Stan Honda/AFP/Getty Images

The photographs in this book are used by permission and through the courtesy of: Getty Images: Junko Kimura, 8, 14; Kochi Kamoshida, 10; Toshifumi Kitamura, 12; Car Culture, 20; Thomas Lohnes, 22; Toru Yamanaka, 24, 25; Fabrice Coffrini, 30; John Moore, 32; Bryan Mitchell, 38; Stan Honda, 41; Ron Kimball/ www.kimballstock.com: 40.
Printed in Malaysia (T)
135642

Contents

Introduction

Most cars in the world run on gasoline, and some cars use more gas than others. Gasoline is made from petroleum, or crude oil, which is a liquid buried deep in the earth. Petroleum formed naturally from the **decomposed** and **compressed** remains of tiny **organisms** that lived millions of years ago. Humans drill deep into the earth to take the oil out.

However, the amount of oil in the world is limited. The more we take out of the ground now, the less there will be in the future, and eventually it will run out. Taking it out of the ground is expensive and damages the **environment**.

Also, when oil and the products made from oil (gasoline, engine oil, heating oil, and diesel fuel) are burned, they give off pollution in the form of gases that damage the **atmosphere**. The carbon dioxide (CO_2) that gasoline-burning engines give off is one of the major causes of **global warming**.

Carbon dioxide is a **greenhouse gas**. Like the glass panes of a greenhouse, the gas traps heat. The build-up of carbon dioxide in the atmosphere, scientists warn, is keeping Earth's heat from escaping into space. As a result, the planet is warming up.

In the United States, about 90 percent of the greenhouse gases we produce is from burning oil, gasoline, and coal. One-third of this comes from the engines that power the vehicles we use to move people and objects around. If we do not stop this global warming, life on Earth could begin to get very uncomfortable.

The problem is not just that temperatures might rise a bit. A warming atmosphere could melt the ice of the Arctic and Antarctic, raise the level of water in the seas, and change the **climate** of many places on Earth. Animals unable to adjust to the new conditions might become extinct (die out). Plants and crops might no longer be able to grow where people need them. Many islands, low-lying countries, and communities along the coasts of all the continents might disappear into the sea.

Doesn't sound so good, does it? These problems are why many people are interested in **alternative fuels** that can power our cars and other engines with less or no pollution.

Now that you know that oil is made from living things that died a long time ago, it should be no surprise that people are making oil from live plants to power their cars. This fuel, called *biodiesel*, can be made from soybean oil, canola oil, sunflowers, and other plants. One form of biodiesel is similar to the vegetable oil used for cooking. Some people gather or buy this used oil from restaurants and use it to power their cars. The engines in these cars have to be modified, or changed, in order to burn this oil correctly.

Another popular way to power cars is with batteries. Modern batteries are being made to be so powerful that some cars use them in combination with gas engines; this system is called *hybrid technology*. Hybrid cars have a gas engine and an electric motor. The electric motor usually takes over when the car runs at low speeds or when it stops.

Many auto engineers are designing electric cars that run only on batteries. Until recently, too many batteries were needed to make this an **efficient** technology. But there have been important advances in battery technology.

Another form of alternative energy for cars is the hydrogen **fuel cell**, which generates power when the hydrogen and oxygen in the fuel cell are combined. If we are to start driving hydrogen-powered cars, however, hydrogen fueling stations would have to be as common along U.S. roads and highways as gas stations are today.

Oil is a limited resource, costs a lot to extract, pollutes the land, air, and water, and forces most countries to rely on the few nations that have a plentiful supply of it. If the world wants to become a cleaner, safer place, developing alternative fuels to power at least some of our vehicles is extremely important.

The Prius is a hybrid vehicle. In fact, it was one of the first hybrids to be sold in America. Since 2000 the Prius has become extremely popular. Drivers like the car because it is not as harmful to the environment as gas-powered vehicles. Because the Prius is partially powered by an electric motor, drivers save money on gas because they do not have to fill up the gas tank as often as with a regular car.

However, while fewer emissions is good, no emissions is even better! Toyota engineers have developed an electric Prius that runs on a battery that can be charged in a standard outlet.

Chapter 1
Green Ideas

Most cars today get between 20 and 25 miles per gallon (8.5 and 10.6 kilometers per liter) of gasoline. The Prius routinely gets 50 miles per gallon (21 km/l), making it one of the most **fuel-efficient** and **environmentally friendly** vehicles in the world.

The secret is the car's **hybrid system**. While most cars are built with a single gasoline engine, the Prius uses both a gas engine and an electric motor. The result is a car that burns less gas than almost every other car on the market. **Manufactured** by Toyota, the Prius is one of the most affordable and best-selling green cars.

◄ **People check out the new, roomier interior of a 2010 Prius. The third-generation hybrid model is the most fuel-efficient Prius yet!**

A NEW GENERATION OF VEHICLES

Even though the Prius is a Japanese-manufactured automobile, in a way the car's story begins in the United States. On September 29, 1993, President Bill Clinton called a press conference to discuss his new program, the Partnership for a New Generation of Vehicles (PNGV). Behind him stood the heads of the "Big Three," America's three major car manufacturers: Chevrolet, Ford, and General Motors (GM).

"Today, we're going to try to give America a new car-crazy chapter in her rich history," Clinton said. The goal of the PNGV, he said, was to "develop affordable, attractive cars that are up to three times more fuel efficient than today's cars."

The second-generation 2003 Prius made a splash in the U.S. market.

The PNGV's main goal was to build a car that got 80 miles per gallon (34 km/l). During the mid-1990s, the PNGV brought together some of the country's leading scientists to work on the project. With the help of the **federal** government, American automakers started engineering what came to be known as the "car of the future."

TOYOTA GETS TO WORK

The Toyota Motor Company faced many difficulties in 1993. With the Japanese economy in a slump, the company's sales were down for the first time in ten years. Partly motivated by Clinton's desire to help American manufacturers build a better car, Toyota vice president Yoshiro Kimbara called upon Toyota's engineers to do the same.

Mission Unaccomplished

For a time, President Clinton's PNGV seemed to be a success. At the 2000 North American International Auto Show, all of the Big Three unveiled **prototypes** of their first green cars. Ford's Prodigy sported rear-facing cameras instead of side-view mirrors to cut down on air resistance. GM's Precept ran on two electric motors. The Dodge ESX3 was made partially out of plastic.

Two years later, the cars were ready to hit the highways. But before they went into production, President George W. Bush canceled the program. Billions of dollars were wasted. The Bush administration instead focused its efforts, and money, on hydrogen fuel-cell technology. Without the monetary support of the government, American automakers were unable to produce their own hybrids with the low gas mileage of their Japanese competitors.

Workers at a Toyota factory assemble 2010 Priuses. Despite a slow economy, demand for the new model was high.

Launching a research commitee called G21 (for "Generation: twenty-first century"), Kimbara wanted his engineers to throw out everything they already knew about making cars and start from scratch. The goals were vague, but Kimbara wanted a new car that was "extremely fuel efficient" and environmentally friendly.

In February 1994 Toyota's engineers got to work. In July they unveiled their plans for a new car that promised an increase in fuel efficiency. But Toyota executives were unhappy. They had asked for a car that would be groundbreaking and had gotten a slightly better version of the same old thing. For a time Toyota engineers were stumped. How could they get significantly better gas mileage out of a standard gas engine? They couldn't.

In late 1994 a Toyota engineer named Masanao Shiomi suggested that the company take a different approach. Forget the gas engine, he said. Toyota's future was in the hybrid system. As a result, Toyota concentrated on developing the technology.

The new and improved hybrid system in the 2010 Prius is on display at a press conference in Tokyo, Japan. The engine *(left)* and the electric motor *(right)* are both under the hood. The battery pack is located in the rear of the car, underneath the trunk.

Chapter 2
Hybrid Technology

Today's third-generation Prius operates with what Toyota calls a Hybrid Synergy Drive system—a fancy way of saying that the car is powered by both a gas engine and an electric motor.

HOW THE PRIUS RUNS

At low speeds the Prius uses only the electric motor that sits under the hood at the front of the car, releasing absolutely no harmful pollutants. When the car travels at speeds faster than approximately 30 miles per hour (48 kilometers per hour), it uses its electric motor in tandem with the gas engine. On the highway, traveling at approximately 60 miles per hour (97 km/h), the gas engine takes over by itself. When the car slows down, it switches back to the electric motor, or EV (electric vehicle) mode. As the Prius stops, the gas engine shuts down completely, saving fuel and protecting the environment.

How does all this work? Under the hood is a Power Control Unit, which houses a series of computers that gauge the speed of the car and switch back and forth between the electric motor and gas engine as needed.

HYBRID HYPE

It took a long time to launch such fuel-efficient and reliable technology. In truth, engineers had been tinkering with hybrid systems since the invention of the automobile in the early twentieth century. However, as the more straightforward, but less environmentally friendly, gasoline engines grew more powerful, experimentation with hybrid systems stopped.

In 1970 a worldwide oil shortage and new American laws calling for cleaner cars renewed interest in the hybrid vehicles. But once the oil crisis passed, experimentation with hybrids stopped again. Finally, as worries about global warming increased in the early 1990s, the hybrid returned—this time to stay.

In early 1995 Toyota put the bulk of its development team's efforts into trying to perfect the hybrid. It was an extremely difficult task, but Toyota executive vice president Akihiro Wada was determined to press ahead quickly, saying:

I don't want simply an extension of past technology. I don't want to build just another economy car. We have to rethink development, and if that means building a hybrid car that gets twice the fuel efficiency as another car out there ... then that's what we'll do.

It was a tall order. Wada wanted a totally new car using totally new technology. To the surprise of Toyota's hardworking engineers, Wada announced that he wanted the hybrid car ready for the next Tokyo Motor Show, which was only a year later.

RUSH TO THE SHOW

As the date of the Tokyo Motor Show approached, Toyota engineers worked around the clock to perfect the new car they had now named Prius, taken from the Latin word meaning "to go before." Designing an engine that worked was one thing. But Toyota engineers also had to resolve problems with the computer system that controlled the car. It was a challenge.

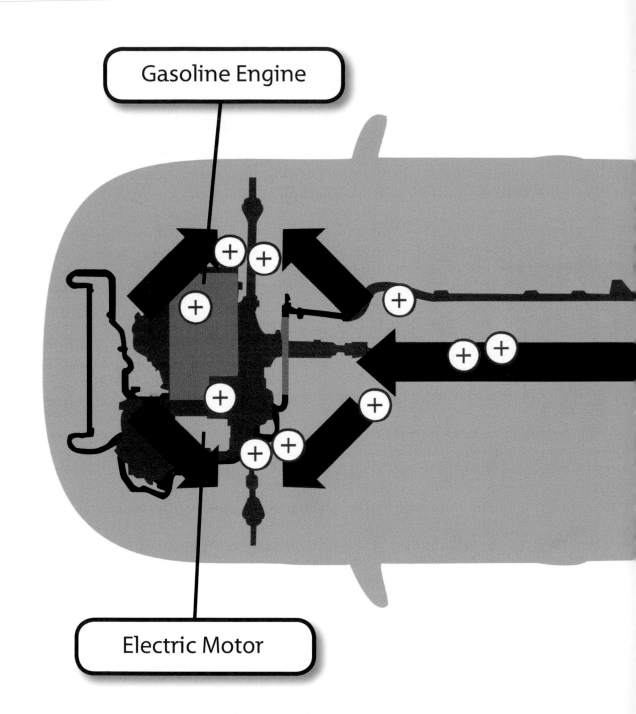

Gasoline Engine

Electric Motor

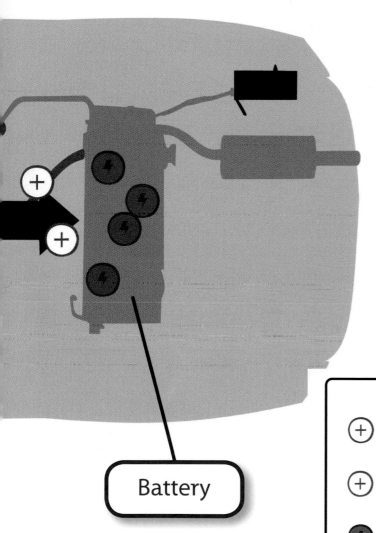

The new hybrid technology in the 2010 Prius draws power from both the gas engine and the electric motor. The battery stores energy from the **regenerative braking** system and from the momentum, or forward motion, of the car as it is being driven.

Battery

Key

⊕ Power from the Electric Motor

⊕ Power from the Gasoline Engine

⚡ Energy being stored in the Battery

Toyota calls its newest hybrid technology package Hybrid Synergy Drive. This cutaway shows what the package, which includes the engine and the motor, looks like before the car body is added.

Building the Right Battery

One of the most difficult challenges faced by Toyota engineers designing the Prius was finding a battery small enough to fit into the body of the vehicle but with enough juice to power the car's electric motor.

In fact, when the first prototype was put on display in 1995, Toyota engineers powered the car with a giant electric condenser, or power source, that stood outside the car itself! Eventually, engineers were able to devise a battery that could fit into the actual car. Not only that, but Toyota engineers designed the hybrid system so that its gas engine recharges the battery pack.

Today, the 2010 Prius features a small battery pack that is housed under the floor behind the rear seat.

At shows and press conferences, the Prius is often displayed with its hood open so that people can see the engine and the motor. Here a photographer snaps a picture at the sixty-first International Motor Show in Frankfurt, Germany, in 2005.

In the early test drives, the software in the car often failed to run. One frustrated engineer complained, "I didn't come to Toyota to work on computers; I came to work on cars." Engineers also had to design a new car body into which the new gasoline engine, electric motor, battery, and computer would fit.

On October 27, 1995, the first Prius prototype debuted at the thirty-first Tokyo Motor Show. In their rush to finish the prototype in time, the Toyota engineers hadn't had time to solve every problem, such as designing a small but powerful battery. Still, boasting 70.56 miles per gallon (30 km/l)—a figure that was wildly inflated—the Prius was a huge hit. Wowed by the car's enormous potential, industry experts overlooked its flaws. Perhaps it really was the car of the future?

Chapter 3
Going Green with the Prius

Despite its promising debut, Prius still had a long way to go before being ready for production. In November 1995 Toyota took the first Prius out for a test drive. Or tried to. Due to a computer glitch, the car didn't move!

And things got worse before they got better. The following February, during another test drive, the car traveled only 500 yards (457 meters) before shutting down. But did that discourage Toyota management? Not at all. The new Toyota president, Hiroshi Okuda, declared that the company needed "to move boldly" to stay at the forefront of hybrid vehicle technology.

◀ **Toyota held a test-drive event in 2009 so that journalists could drive the 2010 Prius before it was put on the market.**

The Celebrities' Choice

When Toyota's engineers were building the Prius, it is doubtful that they knew where they would get their biggest marketing boost: from American movie stars. But in 2002 the *Washington Post* dubbed the Prius "Hollywood's latest politically correct status symbol." It was true. When environmentally conscious film stars such as Leonardo DiCaprio began to drive a Prius, sales went up.

Soon, many Prius buyers were choosing the car as much for its "cool" factor as for its environmentally friendly gas mileage. In 2006 *Washington Post* writer Robert Samuelson coined the term "Prius politics," which referred to a driver's desire to show off and to protect the environment at the same time.

TO THE FINISH LINE

That winter, the Toyota board of directors announced that they wanted the Prius to be available for general purchase in 1997, a year earlier than planned.

But would the car be ready in time? At that point, the Prius battery performance was only half of what was needed. Engineers weren't sure that they could perfect the computer software necessary to run the engine. It wasn't even clear how all the necessary parts would fit into the car! Okuda knew it would be difficult. To help, he put more than half of the company's development team on the Prius project.

Over the next year and a half, Toyota engineers solved the remaining problems one step at a time. After devising a computer that controlled the engine, they finally solved the riddle of the battery, successfully reducing its size. Finally, in August 1997, the car went into production.

That October a model was unveiled at Tokyo's ANA Hotel. As the crowd hushed, chief engineer Takeshi Uchiyamada drove the car from one room to another. Because it was running on electric power, there was no exhaust! Onlookers were impressed. Despite the fact that the car still lacked power—it took thirteen long seconds to accelerate from 0 to 60 miles per hour (0 to 96.5 km/h)—orders poured in.

Designers and engineers often use computer generated images when designing new cars.

THE NEXT GENERATION

In 2003 Toyota introduced its next-generation Prius: a bigger car that promised higher performance at every level. Its most significant improvement was the battery. The voltage was doubled while the weight was reduced, giving the car better acceleration. Under ideal conditions, the car got a remarkable 83.5 miles per gallon (35.5 km/l). In truth, the car's performance during real-road conditions was closer to 50 miles per gallon (21.3 km/l). Best of all, Toyota was able to keep the price the same as it had been in 1997. Sales were tremendous.

But along with Toyota's great success came some problems. In 2005 a handful of American models stalled on the road. That year Toyota sent a team of two hundred software technicians to investigate. They discovered that the problem was caused by a software glitch in some of the cars' computers. In the end, the company agreed to repair approximately 160,000 cars worldwide. A year later, Toyota president Katsuaki Watanabe vowed to redouble efforts to ensure each Prius was in perfect running order.

DRIVING FORWARD

In the summer of 2009 Toyota came out with the 2010 Prius, which was a significant improvement over previous models. The 2010 Prius was more comfortable, more fuel efficient, and, with a new 1.8-liter gasoline engine, more powerful.

Better still, Toyota had added features to make the car more environmentally friendly. Both the front and back headlights now used LED (light-emitting diode) lights, which consume a quarter of the electricity of fluorescent lightbulbs and therefore help reduce the car's electricity consumption and improve fuel efficiency. The body of the car was more **aerodynamic** to reduce wind drag. Running on a more efficient hybrid system, the 2010 Prius was an Advanced Technology Partial Zero Emission Vehicle (AT-PZEV), which means the car produced extremely low levels of smog-forming gases.

Toyota's plug-in Prius concept car was on display at the 2009 Geneva Car Show in Switzerland. Here the car is plugged into an outlet so that people can see how easy it is to charge the battery.

In February 2009 Toyota invited journalists to take the new model for a test drive. One of them was automotive reporter Marty Padgett. He was impressed. "On a total loop of 33.2 miles," he said, "I logged in at 69.5 miles per gallon, without even really trying." As a point of comparison, a 2010 Ford Fusion got 22 miles per gallon in the city and 31 on the highway (9.4 and 13.2 km/l), while a 2010 Saturn Aura got 22 miles per gallon in the city and 33 on the highway (9.4 and 14 km/l).

Toyota advised that most drivers should expect to get approximately 50 miles per gallon (21 km/l). Still, that number was plenty high to rank the Prius as one of the cleanest cars in the world. And **consumers** continued to take notice. Despite a global financial crisis, sales remained strong. As one New York City Prius salesman put it, "We sell them the minute we get them in."

Fun Facts

The 2010 Prius comes with Intelligent Parking Assist, a system that uses sensors in the front bumper to assist the driver in parking the car.

Lane Keep Assist tells the Prius driver when the car is drifting out of its lane.

For safety, the 2010 Prius has a precollision system. When radar on the front grille determines that a collision is unavoidable, precollision brakes are automatically applied and the seat belts automatically retract.

Chapter 4
The Prius of the Future

A current wave in car design is the plug-in: a car that runs on a hybrid system but also has the capability to plug in to an electrical current, such as a wall outlet, increasing battery capacity and allowing the car to travel longer distances using the electric motor alone. After all, the farther a car can travel on electric power, the less gas it uses and the less pollution it produces.

◀ **A woman plugs her Prius PHEV into a solar energy panel (*top left*) at the National Renewable Energy Laboratory (NREL) in Colorado. The laboratory tests and improves solar, wind, and biofuel technology.**

Fun Facts

Moonroofs are cool, but Toyota has managed to make the one on the 2010 Prius even cooler. The optional moonroof has built-in solar panels that are part of the air-circulation system. When the inside of the Prius reaches 86 degrees Fahrenheit (30° Celsius), the Prius uses stored solar energy to power a fan that circulates air to cool the inside so that it is close to the outdoor temperature.

PLUG-IN POWER

Over the past few years, Toyota has been working on the Prius plug-in hybrid electric vehicle (PHEV). In mid-2009 prototypes were traveling 12 miles (19.3 km) on electric power alone. That may not sound like much, but behind the wheel of a Prius PHEV, a driver could conceivably commute a short distance using only electric power—and not pollute the air at all!

Furthermore, companies that modify Priuses to have plug-in capability have sprung up across the country. Many drivers have opted to modify their Priuses so that the cars get more power out of their batteries and electric motors.

Despite the promise of the Prius PHEV, the field of plug-ins is one area in which Toyota seems to be behind its American competitors. Chevrolet plans a late 2010 launch of the Volt, a plug-in that can go 40 miles (64.4 km) on elec-

The moonroof on the 2010 Prius is fitted with solar panels. The solar energy is used to control the car's inside temperature.

tric power without using a drop of gas. Even so, President Obama isn't banking on the Volt to be the car of the future. Because the Volt is priced at $35,000 to $40,000 (the Prius costs around $20,000), the Obama administration worries that it will be "too expensive to be commercially successful in the short term."

THE HOPE OF ETHANOL

Ethanol is a fuel that is produced from materials such as corn, sugar, and cheese. Today, Brazil is the world leader in the production of ethanol-based fuel. But experts say Brazil's natural abundance of sugarcane and its large tracts of farmable land make that country's success difficult to copy. In the United States, ethanol is manufactured from corn, which is mainly grown in Iowa. Critics contend that the energy saved in using the ethanol fuel is canceled out by the enormous amount of energy and natural resources needed to create it. Today, most environmentalists and car experts agree that ethanol is not the magic fuel that people had once hoped it would be.

HYDROGEN CARS

When President Bush canceled the Partnership for a New Generation of Vehicles program, he stressed that the world needed to move beyond gas-powered vehicles to hydrogen cars. In brief, a car powered by hydrogen requires an engine in which hydrogen and oxygen react to produce electricity that is supplied to the motor. There are also hydrogen internal combustion engines, or H2ICEs—these are engines in which hydrogen is burned in a modified gasoline engine.

Though hydrogen cars show promise, there are many hurdles to overcome before they can be manufactured on a large scale.

Aside from making a working engine, engineers need to devise a way to transport the amount of hydrogen required to travel long distances. And as in the production of ethanol, the energy saved in using the new cars must be more than the amount of energy needed to create the hydrogen in the first place. But the biggest hurdle will be setting up a network to fuel the cars. Before hydrogen cars dot America's highways, hydrogen fueling stations will have to be as common as gas stations.

Today, President Obama is steering federal money away from further development of hydrogen cars. Energy Secretary Steven Chu said, "We asked ourselves, 'Is it likely in the next 10 or 15, 20 years that we will convert to a hydrogen car economy?' The answer, we felt, was 'no.'"

LOOKING AHEAD

When President Obama took office in January 2009, American car companies were nearly bankrupt. As part of a bailout package presented to Congress in the spring of that year, the Obama administration tied the federal aid to car companies to a series of tougher environmental standards that manufacturers, included the Big Three, would be expected to follow. Most important, all American cars would be expected to get an average of 35.5 miles per gallon (15.1 km/l) by the year 2016.

A specially painted Prius PHEV was on display at the International Auto Show in Detroit, Michigan, in January 2009. With the advancements being made in battery technology, plug-in vehicles are on the road to success!

At the same time, Congress passed an economic stimulus package that included federal tax breaks of up to $7,500 for a consumer who purchased a plug-in hybrid (such as the Prius PHEV). Though the new federal guidelines might increase the cost of cars by an estimated $600, Obama felt that America was ready to embrace the world of green cars.

I don't accept the conventional wisdom that suggests that the American people are unable or unwilling to participate in a national effort to transform the way we use energy.

In coming years, engineers and scientists will continue to look for new fuels that burn clean, as well as ways to make cars that run farther without producing harmful gases. As research continues, however, more and more companies are following Toyota's lead and making plug-ins and hybrids. General Motors hopes to have twenty-six hybrid models on sale by 2014.

Still, today's hybrid and plug-in market is dominated by Japanese car manufacturers. And one of the most recognizable green cars was the first successful hybrid on the U.S. market: the Toyota Prius.

Vital Stats

1997 PRIUS

Hybrid System Power: 72 hp

Curb Weight: 2,734 lbs (1,240 kg)

Seats: 5

Top Speed: 98.4 mph (158 km/h)

0–60 mph (0–97 km/h): 13 seconds

Average Fuel Economy: 42 mpg (18 km/l)

2010 PRIUS

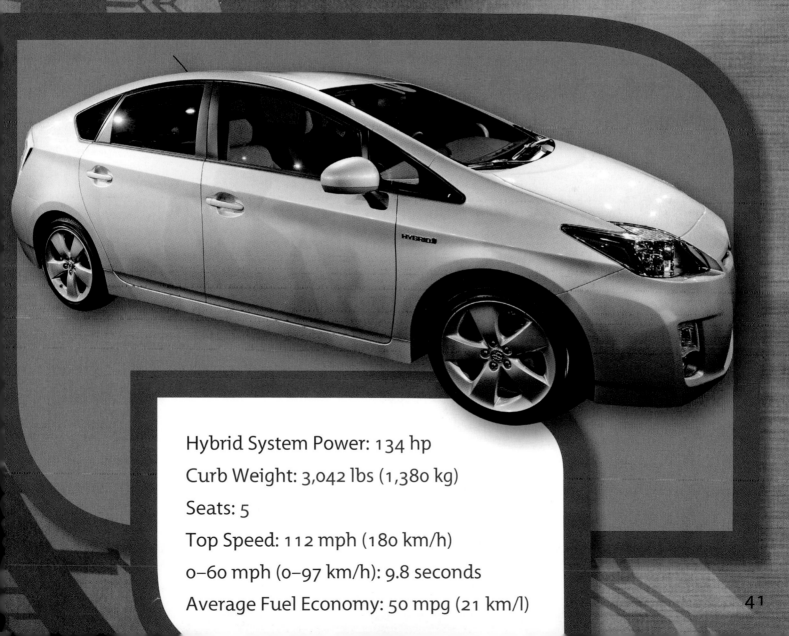

Hybrid System Power: 134 hp

Curb Weight: 3,042 lbs (1,380 kg)

Seats: 5

Top Speed: 112 mph (180 km/h)

0–60 mph (0–97 km/h): 9.8 seconds

Average Fuel Economy: 50 mpg (21 km/l)

41

Glossary

aerodynamic Shaped so that air will easily flow around an object, such as a car, enabling it to go faster with less effort.

alternative fuels Fuels that are less polluting than gasoline is.

atmosphere The air surrounding Earth.

climate The average weather of a place over many years.

compressed Squeezed together; in the case of the life forms that became oil, they were pressed together over millions of years by layers of rock and soil.

consumers People who buy goods and services.

decomposed Broken down into parts; when plants or animals die, they are broken down by time, weather, and the action of insects and bacteria.

efficient Being productive without much waste.

environment The planet's air, water, earth, and living things.

environmentally friendly Cars or technology that make an effort to not pollute the environment.

federal Relating to the national government of the United States, which is made of the executive, legislative, and judicial branches.

fuel cell	A device that changes a chemical fuel, such as hydrogen, into electrical energy, which can power a vehicle.
fuel efficient	Able to travel a longer distance on one gallon of gas than a comparable vehicle.
global warming	An increase in Earth's average yearly temperature, believed to be caused by pollution, that results in climate changes.
greenhouse gas	A gas, such as carbon dioxide, that contributes to global warming.
hybrid system	The combination of a battery-powered electric motor and a gasoline engine used to run a vehicle.
manufactured	Made from materials into a product ready for use.
organisms	Living things.
prototype	The original or model on which something is based or formed.
regenerative braking	A system that changes the heat produced when a car brakes into electricity, which can be stored in the battery.

Further Information

BOOKS

Bearce, Stephanie. *Tell Your Parents All about Electric and Hybrid Cars.* Hockessin, DE: Mitchell Lane Publishers, 2009.

Bradley, Michael. *Prius*. Cars. New York: Marshall Cavendish Benchmark: 2009.

Famighetti, Robert. *How Do Hybrid Cars Work?* Science in the Real World. New York: Chelsea House, 2009.

Juettner, Bonnie. *Hybrid Cars*. Chicago, IL: Norwood House Press, 2009.

Welsbacher, Anne. *Earth-Friendly Design*. Saving Our Living Earth. New York: Lerner, 2008.

WEBSITES

Energy Kids, a website run by the Energy Information Administration, provides information about energy use in the United States.
http://tonto.eia.doe.gov/kids/

Energy Quest is the California Energy Commission's guide to alternative fuel vehicles. There is information on cars that run on gasoline, hydrogen, electricity, and biodiesel, as well as links to sources with more information.
www.energyquest.ca.gov/transportation/

Toyota.com, the official Toyota Prius website, provides information on the newest model and the technology it uses.
www.toyota.com/prius-hybrid

Science News for Kids's article "Ready, Unplug, Drive" has lots of information about plug-in and electric cars.
www.sciencenewsforkids.org/articles/20081029/Feature1.asp

Index

Index

About the Author

Daniel Benjamin is the author of many nonfiction books for younger readers. He lives in New York City with his wife and their two children.